AF271277

Steve McCurry

The Path to Buddha
A Tibetan Pilgrimage

The Path to Buddha
A Tibetan Pilgrimage

The Tibetan boy looks, with inquisitive eyes, directly at us (p.141). He is gazing at Steve McCurry smiling, reverent and intent behind his camera. Although the boy appears brave, he is also like a startled deer, alert to take flight if a tremor feels wrong. He is intensely curious, engaged, wanting to communicate. He stays concentrated, intuits Steve's complex nature; sensing the aesthetic hunter, the discerning eye for form and colour, shape and symmetry and dynamic poise. He senses the energetic professional – he recoils slightly, proud and a touch defiant. He sees a foreigner, a free person outside the control of Chinese masters. Although he still feels fortunate where he is, he wants to reach out to Steve. He sends a fervent message to all who might see him through the camera. We sense a cry for help, a pledge to remain undaunted, a challenge to those who would have him be other than he is.

It is an honour to introduce this luminous collection of Steve's photographs, these precious windows into the Tibetan world through which these brave and beautiful human beings reach out to us by being their open-hearted selves. Path to Buddha it is – a path to Buddha through the human heart, the great heart a people develops from centuries of hard-fought spiritual development and maintains under the terrible duress of colonial occupation.

Who are the Tibetans?
Why 'to Buddha'? Tibetans live in a world where there is a developmental goal, a condition they call 'Buddhahood', which they believe we all are going to reach eventually and where they will have release, happiness, and an abundance of positive energy to share with all those others whom they love – their vast and universal family. Tibetans have achieved something truly remarkable as individuals within a culture. They have gone beyond most forms of ancestor worship, so powerful in most other cultures of this world and once so for them. We are drawn to them because they see us as familiar, potentially a relative, a friend; they emanate a sense of already being familiar with us.

To understand the Tibetans, it is first necessary to dispel erroneous preconceptions about them. At one extreme, some people think of Tibet as 'Shangri-La', a paradise where no one suffers or grows old, a place of mystical beings who are wise and gentle. This comes from Tibet's remoteness, which has allowed travellers to project their wildest fantasies upon it, and also from the fact that the tall Himalayas and the other mountain chains that surround the three-mile-high Tibetan plateau are thought of as the abodes of deities by the lowland peoples of India, China and Central Asia. In his novel *Lost Horizon* (1933), James Hilton invented the name 'Shangri-La' for his Tibetan utopia, and the fantasy was further popularized in the West by the film version of the book. The 'Shangri-La' image of Tibetans as other-worldly creatures has been generally overcome by several generations of scholarly investigations and publications, well-informed popular accounts, books by the Tibetans themselves, and hundreds of thousands of travellers actually visiting Tibet. So people are more or less ready to encounter Tibetans as regular human beings, with real suffering and real beauty, and a special quality of joyfulness even under duress.

At the other extreme, however, we 'moderns' have the idea that anyone living in a country without an industrial infrastructure, without universal education, mostly without electricity, is 'primitive', with an intriguing quality of exotic, 'barbaric splendour', charming, perhaps fascinating, but out of touch with modern 'reality', a relic. In the case of Tibet, this standard 'primitive' image has been intensified and complicated by over fifty years of Communist propaganda, itself built upon centuries of suspect missionary accounts of Tibetan idolatry, demon-worship, and so on. On top of being generally primitive and barbaric, the Communists represent Tibet as medieval, a harsh and cruel land of feudal serfdom, its people trapped by a superstitious religion under an oppressive theocracy. The 'feudal theocracy' image is still intact, consciously or unconsciously as the case may be, because people want to ignore the reality of the Tibetan genocide and owing to mixing the images of 'medieval feudalism' with more current images of 'backwardness' and 'underdevelopment'.

It takes a critical effort to relieve ourselves of this 'primitive' or 'pre-modern' stereotype and open our minds to new notions such as 'non-industrial modernity', 'non-materialist rationality', and so forth. To stir a deeper appreciation of these photographic encounters with individual members of a people, it is helpful to entertain the notion of the Tibetan as an unexpected, new type of person: neither a Shangri-La mystic nor a backward primitive; and not just like us, a 'modern', post-industrial, secular citizen, either. The Tibetan tends to be a highly individualistic person who yet enacts a natural, easy altruism, cheerful under pressure, gentle, easy-going in relating to others, tolerant and slow to violence, and aware of the spiritual aspect of life without losing the earthiness of simple pleasures. Are these apparent qualities simply innate in Tibetans? Natural, from their landscape, soaring summits, the high altitude, the vast wide-open spaces? No, their special qualities are a product of their long immersion in the Buddhist culture, of their thousand-year-long struggle to overcome their early horrific militarism and attendant social violence, and to develop the profound introspective insight that is the aim of the Buddhist education.

What is 'Tibet?'

'Tibet' is not the country's indigenous name. Its own name is 'Boeud' and a 'Tibetan' is a 'Boeupa'. Indians in the Himalayas have called the land 'Bhotia' for thousands of years. 'Tibet' came about from the Mongolians, who picked up the Tibetan word for northern Tibet, 'Toeu Boeut' ('Upper Tibet'), and then shared this with Arabic-speaking people who called it 'Tubbat', and so on into English. The key to seeing what is Tibet is to look at a relief map of Asia. Right in the middle, above India, west of China, east of Afghanistan, south of the Gobi desert, a high plateau sticks up above everything, the ring of mountains around it like petals of a flower. It is almost a million square miles, bigger than the Indian subcontinent or the size of all of Western Europe. It is deeply crevassed by the beds of all of Asia's great rivers. Looking at the map, you can see the natural boundary following a line of around 10,000 feet, about two miles high, with the plateau averaging three miles in altitude. That huge entity is Tibet.

Tibet has always been sparsely populated as much of it is high desert and the steppes, although verdant, are too high for mechanized farming and therefore can support only livestock, sustaining a semi-nomadic, pastoral lifestyle. No vast waving fields of grain there – just delicate wild grasses pleasing to the yaks, antelopes and wild donkeys. Its native population is around six million.

The Chinese creation called the 'Tibet Autonomous Region' (TAR) is about one third of geographical and historical Tibet, and contains only one third of the Tibetan people. The other two thirds live to the east in the 'Tibetan Autonomous Prefectures' (TAPs) of the neighbouring Chinese provinces of Qinghai, Gansu, Sechwan and Yunnan. Presently, what used to be Tibet's towns, now cities, are swollen with around ten million Chinese colonists, mostly in the TAPs – huddling together in the frontier-worker barrack cities filled with cheap concrete structures. There is no coal or firewood in most of Tibet for the long cold winters, so rivers are dammed and ancient glacial lakes are drained to provide electricity for these crowded urban hives.

The Tibetans now live mostly in the countryside, where they have always thrived – except when coping with foreign incursions, which were brief owing to the natural obstacle of the altitude. In their own version of history, they unified most of the plateau during the early Common Era centuries, finishing the job by creating a single imperial country governing the entire plateau in the sixth century CE. They then turned their strength and enterprise towards amassing more wealth by conquering their neighbours, becoming unstoppable in their violent progress during the seventh to ninth centuries. To keep the Tibetan armies away, the Chinese emperors, Nepali kings, and other smaller rulers of that period made tribute payments to the Tibetan emperor.

Tibet controlled the Silk Route and its lucrative trade for about two centuries. Fortunately for their neighbours, they had little impulse to settle down in any region below 10,000 feet: they simply raided and spread fear, exacted tribute, and returned to their high plateau.

During this period they also came in contact with Buddhism, not just a 'religion' but rather the cultural matrix of all the advanced countries around Tibet at this time. The emperors decided to import Buddhism's universalizing philosophy to raise the ethical, intellectual and spiritual level of their subjects, in spite of the contradiction between Buddhism's teaching of non-violence and the empire's need for violence in order to maintain its power. The people responded positively after some time, no doubt relieved to be spared some of the more strenuous imperial adventures, and despite some resistance from the feudal lords the Buddhist way of life began gradually to supplant in their minds the previous tribal and imperial ones.

The period from around 1000 to 1400 saw a gradual transformation of Tibet into a zone of Buddhist practice, the monastic institution at the heart of that social style becoming inexorably more and more central in the lives of the people. There was an intense period of popular, mass mystic experience in around 1400, when a social lifestyle focused on Buddhist personal evolution as the main purpose of human life became formally enshrined at the heart of Tibetan society. The Great Prayer Festival was founded in 1409, marking an event in Shakyamuni Buddha's biography when the spiritual power of enlightenment became manifest in a public triumph over the material powers of the world. Huge monastic universities were built in Lhasa, the combined populations of which exceeded the population of the town. The monasticization of Tibet accelerated even more after that, until in the sixteenth and seventeenth centuries the aristocratic descendants of the old imperial warlords saw their power base in land, wealth, people and ideology dissolving once and for all. Alarmed by this, the more ambitious

of these lords decided to stand and fight, to crush the people's obsession with monastic other-worldliness that was fatal to their power. The final assault by the aristocratic lords took place during the youth of the Fifth Dalai Lama, Losang Gyatso (1617-82), but he turned the tables on them and ended up, in 1642, consolidating social, political and spiritual power in a unique new government, in which sacred and secular were coordinated in favour of the sacred.

This event can be considered the birth of Tibet as a society committed to maximize inner development through systematic self-conquest. The Ganden Palace government of Tibet of the last three and a half centuries changed society from a communal, feudal society to a more individualistic, mass society, with a bureaucratically governed, centralized tax system grounded in free peasant ownership of land. It demilitarized the aristocratic warlords, changed their previous feudal land-ownership to a moderate tax-entitlement, and enlisted them as servants of the state. They worked in offices in formal collaboration with monastic officials in bureaux of treasury, foreign affairs, education, justice, and so on. The government placed the bulk of the national budget at the service of the great monastic universities, making lifelong spiritual education the central and most meaningful concern of the nation. The entire seasonal cycle of all the people was seamlessly woven around the great purpose of life, to evolve towards enlightenment to the fullest of one's capacity.

This was the modern Tibet that could so easily be confused with a feudal society, since the infrastructure had been purposely kept at a technologically intermediate stage, wheels being mainly used for prayer machines, not for transport or factory machinery. This was the modern Tibet that accomplished the unique social feat that all the world's people long for seemingly in vain today – the overall demilitarization of culture and society. This was the modern Tibet that released any individual so motivated to pursue for the sake of self and others his or her highest intellectual, spiritual and evolutionary aspirations for higher

being. This was the modern Tibet that produced the people we meet in Steve's photographs.

What is Buddhism?

Buddhism grew from the great enlightenment and teaching of the Shakya Prince Siddhartha, who thereby became the Shakyamuni Buddha. His enlightenment was not an encounter with a creator god. In fact, it involved his critical rejection of the very idea of such an omnipotent being. He was unlike most religious founders in that he had no mission to save beings from suffering by getting them to believe in the saving power of a god. Nor did he pretend he could save them. His good news was that they could ultimately save themselves from all suffering, enjoy perfect bliss forever and share it with all others, by understanding fully their own real nature and the reality of all things. He saw that all beings have the capacity for omniscience, although they need to evolve greatly to fulfil it. What they must do is to educate themselves to develop their understanding. This insight of the Buddha compelled him to become primarily an educator. His Dharma (way to perfect truth) was a higher education for people in ethics, heart/mind and critical wisdom. The first spawned the ethical and legal patterns of the numerous Buddhist civilizations, the second the religions, and the third the sciences, the most important ones being philosophy and psychology.

Almost all Tibetans feel highly fortunate to live in what they call a 'central' country, where the Buddha Dharma is at the centre of life. They preferably make their lives most meaningful by becoming monk or nun, opting out of reproduction and production responsibilities in order to focus full-time on self-transformation for the sake of all beings. Here it must be clear that one becomes a Buddhist renunciate not merely to retreat into silence and prayer in worship of a deity, but to re-educate oneself critically and meditationally from the intellect to the instincts, in order to transcend the self-centred perception and habit of the ordinary human animal, and become a Bodhisattva, a higher being of self-fulfilment through wisdom and other-fulfilment through compassion. This self-transformative evolution as the purpose of life was the reason why Tibet developed its unique 'mass monastic' society, with its huge number of monasteries and monastic universities, housing up to twenty per cent of the population, supported by a large proportion of the national budget. But even if they spend their lives as a simple peasant or nomad, child, father, mother, brother, sister, friend, devotee, they feel close to the possibility of themselves eventually engaging in such evolutionary education, gain great merit by supporting those who are engaged in it, and aim by their deeds to become a full-time monastic practitioner in a proximate future life.

Meeting the exceptional individuals in this book
The monks and nuns in these pictures are joyous and energized because they are fortunate enough to be supported by their peers in devoting their core life energies to the pursuit of enlightenment and its happiness and freedom, irrespective of whether they are in exile or under occupation. The Tibetan people as a whole have been wrestling for several generations now with the incomprehensibility of another people coming into their blessed land and turning it from a theatre of personal evolution into a vale of needless suffering – and all under the banner of improving the quality of material life. By contrast, when modern Tibet made spiritual life the central concern, the quality of material life took care of itself with relatively little stress. When the Communists used force to cast away all spiritual activities as feudal or bourgeois delusions, the material necessities – personal possessions, religious treasures, houses, monasteries, ornate inherited furnishings, livestock, cultivated fields – all were righteously destroyed as reminding the Tibetans of their supposedly backward culture. Today, with the intensive Chinese colonization more than doubling the population of geographic Tibet, the fragile high-altitude land has become overstressed, environmentally damaged in all respects, in spite of the unnatural loss of over a million Tibetans.

As I look at Steve's portraits, I can enter into a dialogue in Tibetan with any of his subjects. He has a way of presenting himself as opening an honest channel for them to contact the vast potential of others. The old monk stands there in the first picture (p.11) battered but unbowed. He stands in the Jokhang Temple in Lhasa, built in the seventh century by Songzen Gambo (c. 593-649), the first great 'Dharma Emperor', who inherited and expanded the empire and first founded Buddhist Tibet. In the centre of that temple there is an image of Shakyamuni Buddha that Tibetans believe was made when the Buddha was alive, a true portrait. It was destroyed by Chinese soldiers in 1959, but pieces were hidden and later retrieved and put back together in the 1980s. The old monk stands with that sacred icon, Tibet's warrant that the Buddha is always with them, no matter what, from life to life, with death nothing more than a transit from one worn-out body to another better vessel for enlightenment evolution. The old monk stands there, his face amazingly wrinkled and relaxed, a comfortable leather mask, bronzed by the powerful Tibetan sun on the limitless steppes he has crossed to reach this holiest of places in Tibet. He is not from Lhasa, he has come from afar as a pilgrim. He seems concerned, not angry, not resentful, enduring, forbearing, yet also questioning. 'Why has this been necessary? What more is there to come? Whatever it is, we can bear it. We will be here. We are real. We also know we dream, and, by the blessings of the Three Jewels, the Buddha, his teaching, his community, we know we will awaken some day, some life or another. OM MANI PADME HUM — Hail to the Jewel Lotus Lord of Compassion!'

Steve McCurry's photographs are born out of his respect for the existential fact of these Tibetan human beings, individual by individual. That is the greatness of his art: his honesty, courage, and truth meeting those of his subjects. Enjoy these treasures. Take time with them. Go on pilgrimage with them. Find their path to Buddha.

Portraits

Monk at the Jokhang
Temple in Lhasa

Woman at the Ganden
Monastery near Lhasa

Woman in the Barkhor
quarter of Lhasa

Pilgrim at the Sera
Monastery in Lhasa

Pilgrim in Lhasa

Woman from Amdo
province in Lhasa

Carpet dealer in the
main bazaar in Kandze

Pilgrims

Young boy walks through
barley fields near Kandze

Families drinking and
preparing tea in their
homes in Amdo province
and in the town of Shigatse

Nomads in their tent
made from coarse yak
wool, near Manigango

Pilgrims making circuits round
the Drepung Monastery, outside
Lhasa, and in Amdo province,
an act that Buddhists believe
will bring them good karma

Mother carrying her child through
Barkhor, the last traditional Tibetan
quarter of Lhasa

In Lhasa, nomads from
Amdo province wait to
enter the Jokhang Temple
– considered to be the
most holy site in Tibet

Mother and child at the
horse festival in Tagong

Man walking through the
Barkhor quarter of Lhasa

Pilgrim circumambulating
the monastery at Tagong

Pilgrims travel across Tibet on
horseback, yaks – the traditional
method of travelling in Tibet –
and on foot. These pilgrims are
in Drango and Amdo province

Pilgrims circumambulating
the monastery at Labrang and
the Jokhang Temple in Lhasa

Nomad woman in her
yak-hair tent, Kham province

Mother and child walking
through the streets
in Kham province

In Lithang a woman carries
a Mani stone decorated
with mantras

Schoolboy in Lhasa
posing for his picture

Pilgrims approaching
the monastery in Lithang

Amdo nomads in a tent and in
a photographic studio in Lhasa

At a horse festival in Tagong,
locals observe the activities,
while a young couple proudly
pose for their photograph

提高民
旅 贡

Pilgrim at the Drango Monastery
in Kham province

Traditional Chinese Daoist doctor
diagnosing a patient while two
others wait. He plies his trade in
front of a sign that reads 'Improve
the quality of nationalities'

Pilgrim resting in Dranang at the
Samye Monastery, which is the
oldest monastery in Tibet. *Samye*,
means 'unimaginable' in Tibetan.

Pilgrims waiting to enter the
Jokhang Temple in Lhasa

Family having tea in Tagong

Devotees prostrating themselves outside the Jokhang Temple, Lhasa. Some devotees aim to complete up to 100,000, or more, prostrations during their lifetime

Woman praying in front of the
Potala in Lhasa – the former home
of the Dalai Lamas, and at one
time Tibet's seat of government
and a religious centre

Man praying ouside the
Jokhang Temple, Lhasa.
His prayer wheel, in front of
him, contains many rolls of
paper printed with prayers

Group of devotees prostrating
their way to Lhasa. It will take
them two years to get there

Devotee worshipping at
Bodh Gaya, India. According to
Buddhist belief it was here that
the Buddha, after sitting for
several days under the Bodhi tree,
attained spiritual enlightenment

Pilgrim praying at the
Buddhist academy of
Larung Gar in Kham province

Prayer flags, such as these in
Lhasa, are hung outside so the
wind can carry the prayers through
the air and down the streets, where
devotees pray in the early morning

Prayer flags, hung to bring
happiness and prosperity,
cover a hillside in Machen

Giant silk *thangka* being unrolled
on a hillside for a festival at the
Drepung Monastery outside Lhasa.
The monastery was damaged
during the Cultural Revolution

Portraits

Man in a tea shop in Derge

Woman in the Barkhor
quarter of Lhasa

Woman at horse
festival in Tagong

Woman at horse
festival in Tagong

Young pilgrim at the
monastery in Labrang

Young woman at
the Potala in Lhasa

Worshipper at temple in Batang

Monks

Young *Tulku* in a tea shop
in Bodh Gaya, India. *Tulku*
is the Buddhist term used
to describe the reincarnation
of a spiritual leader

Cola
Cola

Pilgrim praying with monks
at the Buddhist academy of
Larung Gar, Kham province

Monk outside the monastery
at Labrang, formerly the
home of 5,000 monks but
now housing about 500

Monks travelling by foot through
Drango and on horseback
in Sershul. They are going
to town to say prayers

A monk marks his arrival from
his pilgrimage with a photograph
in a local studio near Jyekundo

Monks debating in a monastery in
Amdo province, and parading in a
ceremonial procession in Labrang

Monks protesting in Dharamsala
in Northern India, the home
of the Dalai Lama in exile

Monks gathering at the academy
of Larung Gar, Kham province

Debates, such as this at a
monastery in Bylakuppe, India,
form an important part of a
Buddhist monk's education

Monks watching the preparations
for the yoghurt festival at the
Drepung Monastery, outside Lhasa

Young monks studying
in Lithang

Monk meditating in
a monastery in Sakya

Monks saying prayers in a
nomad tent in Amdo province

Novice monk studying in a
monastery in Amdo province

Nomad altar in a tent in Kham
province showing a picture
of the Dalai Lama, whom
Tibetan Buddhists regard
as their spiritual leader

Monks begin their training
at an early age, such as
these novices in Machen

Monks at rest and studying in
Bylakuppe, India and Machen

A monk prays while a nun
lights candles at a Tibetan prayer
festival in Bodh Gaya, India

Young *Rinpoche* in a monastery
in Sakya. *Rinpoche* means
'precious' in Tibetan

Novice monk studying in Lithang

Monks prostrating themselves at a
prayer festival in Bodh Gaya, India

Candles are a form of offering at the
Tibetan prayer festival in Bodh Gaya,
India, during which thousands are lit
under the Bodhi tree

Student at monastery school
in Amdo province and monk
outside the academy of Larung Gar,
Kham province, offering prayers

A monk reads alone before
a poster of the alps in Ganden
Monastery, near Lhasa, while
monks in the Drepung Monastery,
outside Lhasa, meditate together

Monks prostrate themselves
while circumambulating the Bodhi
tree at Bodh Gaya, India. Such
circuits are completed clockwise

Young monk holding flowers to
be offered in prayer at the academy
of Larung Gar, Kham province

Portraits

Woman at horse festival, Tagong

Woman at horse festival, Tagong

Village girl from Kham
province at a festival

Girl in new Chinese coat, Shigatse

Nomad boy in Manigango

Nomad boy at the
monastery in Lithang

Nomad boy in yak-hair
tent, Amdo province

Acknowledgements

For Pamela

Bill Allen
Anna Marie Baker
Michael Carroll
His Holiness the Dalai Lama
Neha Diddee
John Echave
Charlotte Garner
Jackson
Audrey Jonckheer
Kent Kobersteen

Elizabeth Krist
Sarah Mclaughlin
Marla Mossman
Deepak Puri
Amanda Renshaw
Richard Schlagman
Lou Simons
Susan Smith
Tenzin Taklha
Robert Thurman
Bonnie V'Soske
Danette Walker